Let's Read About...
César Chávez

To Marcos, Renee, Emilio . . .
and all the people in the fields
who work to bring food to our tables.
—J.T.

To Ms. Rallou Hamshaw, who many years
ago, gave me my first illustration assignment,
and made sure I did it correctly.
—S.M.

ISBN 0-439-68051-4

Text copyright © 2004 by Jerry Tello.
Illustrations copyright © 2004 by Stephen Marchesi.

All rights reserved. Published by Scholastic Inc.

SCHOLASTIC, CARTWHEEL BOOKS, and associated logos are trademarks and/or registered trademarks of Scholastic Inc.

20 21 22 23 24/0

Printed in the U.S.A. 40
First printing, October 2004

Let's Read About...
César Chávez

Scholastic
First Biographies

by Jerry Tello

Illustrated by Stephen Marchesi

Cartwheel
·B·O·O·K·S·®

SCHOLASTIC INC.

New York   Toronto   London   Auckland   Sydney
Mexico City   New Delhi   Hong Kong   Buenos Aires

César Estrada Chávez was born
on March 31, 1927.
He lived with his family
in a small house in Arizona.

César's family needed to move
to California to find work.
This is where César started school.

School was hard for César.
He spoke Spanish.
His teachers spoke English.
They had trouble understanding each other.

But César loved to learn.
He learned an important lesson
from his mother.
She told him that all people deserved respect.

César's family traveled all over California to work.
They would pick fruits and vegetables
in the fields.
César would go to whatever school was nearby.
He went to 37 different schools
by the time he was in eighth grade!

César had to leave school to work in the fields.
He needed to help his family make money.
César worked from morning until night.
He saw the landowners treat the workers very badly.
This went against his mother's lesson of respect.

César joined the Navy when he was 17 years old.
He was sad to leave his family.
He sent money home to help them.
César never forgot the hard life in the fields.

Many years passed.
César went home to California in 1948.
He met a young woman named Helena Fabela.
They fell in love and soon got married.

César and Helena taught field workers
to read and write.
They hoped that this would help the workers
speak up for their rights.

César started a group to help
the workers even more.
It was called the United Farm Workers.
César traveled to many farms.
He would talk to the workers
about their need to be treated fairly.

The group decided to make a flag.
It was red and black.
It had an eagle on it.
It stood for the pride and courage
of the workers.

The group went on marches and strikes.
The landowners ignored César and the workers.
They said they would fire the workers
if they did not stop marching and striking.

The workers became very angry.
César decided he needed to do more.
He fasted for 25 days.
That means he did not eat any food.
César did this to make people see he was serious.

César and his group fought hard for change.
He wanted respect for the people
who worked hard in the fields every day.

Today, there are schools, streets, and libraries
named in honor of César Chávez.
He spent his life fighting to help others.
César Chávez is a hero to us all.

THE

EVERYTHING®

GUIDE TO

WORKING WITH ANIMALS

From dog groomer to wildlife rescuer—tons of great jobs for animal lovers

Michele C. Hollow and William P. Rives, VMD